One Big Flathead

by **Peter Matheson**
Illustrated by **Stephen Axelsen**

Chill Out is published by Nelson Thomson Learning and is distributed as follows:

AUSTRALIA
Nelson Thomson Learning
102 Dodds Street
Southbank 3006
Victoria

NEW ZEALAND
Nelson Price Milburn
1 Te Puni Street
Petone
Wellington

First published in 2002
10 9 8 7 6 5 4 3 2 1
05 04 03 02

Text © Peter Matheson 2002
Illustrations © Stephen Axelsen 2002

One Battered Flathead
ISBN 0 17 010 525 3

Project commissioned and managed by Lorraine Bambrough-Kelly,
The Writer's Style
Designed by Karen Mayo
Series design by James Lowe
Illustrations by Steve Axelsen
Printed in China by Midas Printing (Asia) Ltd

Acknowledgements

Thank you to the teachers and students of St John's Primary School, Heidelberg; St Francis Xavier Primary School, Montmorency; Luther College, Wonga Park; and the Atchison and Burns families. Thanks also to Lynn Howie and the Stage 3 boys at Alstonville Primary School for their assistance in developing this series.

Nelson Australia Pty Limited ACN 058 280 149 (incorporated in Victoria) trading as Nelson Thomson Learning.

Contents

Chapter 1	**Battered**	5
Chapter 2	**Bullied**	13
Chapter 3	**Bravado**	17
Chapter 4	**Bribes**	25
Chapter 5	**Blessing**	31
Chapter 6	**Beginnings**	37

CHAPTER 1

Battered

'You can't get away, Flathead. We're right behind you,' Con heard Mad Dog yell over the rumble of their skateboards.

Con saw Mad Dog, Jonno and Sass getting closer. He tried to run faster. He hoped they wouldn't hurt him as much as they did last time. He hoped that they wouldn't rip his shirt again.

He ran into the underground car park. And ducked behind the cars. He hoped to throw them off in the dark. It didn't work.

They caught him in the shadows. At the bottom of the ramp to the shops.

Con curled into a ball. He tried to protect himself from the kicks and the punches. Mad Dog held Con down. And the other two laid into him.

'What's going on here?' A male voice boomed from the ramp.

Con could hear Mad Dog, Jonno and Sass scattering.

Footsteps thumped towards him. Firm hands pulled him to his feet.

'Are you all right, boy?' The man brushed at Con's shirt.

Con looked into the face of Mr Panakos, the maths teacher.

Mr Panakos looked around the car park. And saw the boys rolling away on their skateboards. He turned to Con. 'I know you. You're Constantine Dimitriades, year seven?'

Con nodded.

'Who did this to you?' Con shook his head. If he dobbed on Mad Dog, there'd be even bigger trouble.

Mr Panakos crossed his arms. 'See me tomorrow at school, Constantine. First thing.'

CHAPTER 2

Bullied

Con's mother threw the hot chips onto the paper and wrapped them. Con pushed his way through the crowd in their shop, The Fisherman's Basket. He came home now, because he knew the shop would be very busy. And his mother wouldn't see another tear in his shirt.

Con walked quickly through the shop to his room. He turned the music up real loud.

Later, after the evening rush had died down, his mother came into his bedroom. She noticed the rip in his shirt. 'What happened? Who did this? Have you been fighting again?' His mum went on and on.

Somehow, it all fell out of his mouth. He told her how a few weeks ago he had upset Mad Dog. Then Mad Dog thumped him. And started stealing his things.

Jonno and Sass joined in. They started following him. Every time he turned around they were watching him. He knew if he ratted on them, they'd bash him.

Last week after school they chased him. Just recently they gave him a ten second start.

His mother's eyes grew angry. 'Stand up to these bullies, Con. If you turn and run, they'll think you're a coward.'

She told him that all bullies were cowards. And that if he faced them, *they* would turn and run. All Con had to do was tell them he wasn't scared.

Chapter 3

Bravado

'One. Two. Three...'

He heard the counting as soon as he stepped out of the school gate.

Mad Dog stood leaning against the gatepost. Jonno was sitting on his skateboard and smirked.

'I'm not scared of you, Mad Dog.'

Mad Dog stepped close to him. Jonno stood closer. 'Glad to hear it, Flathead.'

Mad Dog pushed Con towards Jonno. 'You've still got seven seconds.'

'Your fun's over, Mad Dog,' Con yelled.

Mad Dog laughed, 'It's only just started. Four. Five…'

Con turned and ran.

Con didn't hear Mr Panakos call out, 'Matthew Trantor and Jonathan Jones, just the people I want to see.'

But he did wonder why he wasn't chased that afternoon. And his mother beamed at seeing his shirt in one piece.

Later that afternoon, he helped in the shop. Mad Dog and Sass came in and ordered chips. They sweet-talked his dad. But gave Con the evil eye.

His dad suggested Con go out and muck around with the nice boys. He was surprised when Con didn't want to.

His grandfather came into his room after dinner. He had seen Mad Dog in the shop and didn't like the look of him.

He told Con there was more than one way to beat the enemy. His grandfather told him that during the war, he made friends with the enemy. He gave them things. And then tricked them.

The next morning, Con took a packet of cigarettes and some cola from his parents' shop. Then went to school.

After morning break, he had to go and see Mr Panakos.

'You forgot to see me yesterday, Constantine. Any reason?'

Con shook his head.

Mr Panakos asked if he knew Matthew Trantor and Jonathan Jones from year nine.

Con shook his head again. But wondered how much the dark eyes knew.

'Promise you will see me if it happens again?'

Con nodded.

But he didn't keep the promise.

CHAPTER 4

Bribes

'One. Two. Three…'

Con pulled out three bottles of cola. He handed them to Mad Dog, Jonno and Sass.

'You trying to bribe us?' Mad Dog asked.

'What else you got?' Jonno sneered. Sass took Con's bag and up-ended it. The cigarettes fell out.

'What are these?' Sass asked.

'Mine!' Jonno scooped them up. The three boys passed the cigarettes around.

'You get these from home?' Sass asked.

Con nodded. 'They're a peace offering.'

Mad Dog pointed towards the school gates. And quick as a flash, the cigarettes disappeared.

Mr Panakos walked out of the gates. He stopped when he saw the boys.

He stepped over to them. 'It's strange seeing you three hanging around with a year seven boy. What is going on here, Trantor?'

Mad Dog looked innocent. 'Nothing, Mr Panakos.'

Mr Panakos caught Con's eye. 'There better not be, Trantor. Are you all right, Dimitriades?'

Con nodded. And Mr Panakos walked off.

Mad Dog leant close to Con. 'Tomorrow there had better be two packets.' He smiled at the other two. 'What number was I up to?'

'Four,' said Jonno.

Con picked up his bag and ran.

CHAPTER 5

Blessing

His grandmother pulled out a small bag that was hanging on a string round her neck.

She took out a battered white stone. And pressed it into Con's hand.

'It comes from the old country,' she said.

It was flat and shaped like a fish. There was a hole for an eye. And a string through its mouth.

'It's a special stone that protects you in war. I get it from my grandmother. I give it to grandfather for his war. It saved him. And then I give it to your father, when he was in danger. It saved him, too.'

She tied it round Con's neck. It felt flat and cool against his skin. 'Now it protects you in your war.' His grandmother looked proudly at him.

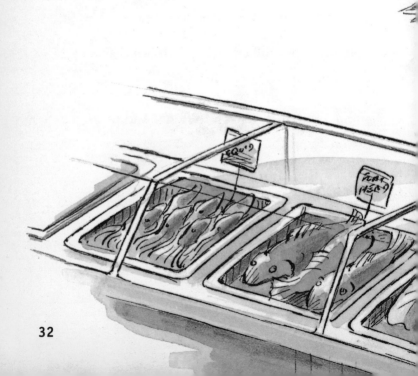

His grandfather saw the fish stone and smiled.
He told Con that in his town in the old country, this
fish was special. It was fast, clever and hard to catch.

His father nodded as he lowered a piece of flathead
in batter into the oil. He smiled, too.

The phone rang in the shop. His mother answered. 'Mr Panakos? What's wrong? Is Con in trouble?' Her eyes scowled at Con. 'I will come and see you after school tomorrow.'

CHAPTER 6

Beginnings

'One. Two. Three…'

Con swung round and pressed the fish stone close to his chest. The fish seemed to flip under his fingers.

'Flathead. Where's the smokes? Give 'em to me,' Mad Dog demanded.

Con stood his ground. The fish seemed to flop against his heart. He took a deep breath. He thought of the fish protecting him. It was fast, clever, hard to catch. 'I'm not doing this anymore,' he said firmly.

'Fine by me.' Mad Dog swung his fist at Con's head. Con ducked. 'Get him,' yelled Mad Dog.

Jonno and Sass stepped in. But somehow Con side-stepped them both.

Con ran. But today it felt different. He felt different. He slipped through the air like a fish through water.

And the three boys, who chased him, stumbled and staggered.

Laughing, he led them away from the school.

He darted through the car park.

He dashed round the block. Then back to school. His mother was at the school gates talking to Mr Panakos.

He ran up to them and stopped.

Mad Dog, Jonno and Sass flapped up. Sweating. Puffing.

Mr Panakos turned and said, 'Well, look what we've caught here!'

Author Snapshot
Peter Matheson

I was lucky at school. I survived. But I learnt very early how to become very quiet, especially with bullies lurking nearby. I lost it, just once (about when this picture was taken). A boy a year or two above me was hassling a little old lady at a bus stop.
I opened my mouth too wide and got a bleeding nose, busted lip and torn shirt.

And it hasn't changed. I see my son getting into fights because some bully needs to prove something.

We need the RSPAB (Royal Society for Protection Against Bullies) and if that isn't around when you read this, talk to your dad, your mum, a teacher, the principal, anyone close to you, and get one organised.

Peter Matheson as a teenager

Illustrator Snapshot
Stephen Axelsen

How should we deal with bullies? Some people learn kung fu. Others make sure that their friends are slow runners. They can leave them behind as bully distractions. Being invisible is useful too. If I sensed bullies on the prowl, I would become so quiet and dull that danger would pass me by.

But if kung fu, slow friends and being invisible aren't going to work, I think it is best to get help from a mum, a dad, a teacher, and the RSPAB (Royal Society for Protection Against Bullies).

Stephen Axelsen as a teenager

Read **These**

Urgent Delivery by Dianne Bates

Revenge at Lake Happy by Jim Schembri

Private Keep Out by Christopher Stitt

A Prize Idiot by Bill Condon

In the Can by Christopher Stitt

The Reef Riders by Corinne Fenton

Fangs by Dianne Bates

Tag Dag by Christopher Stitt

Pitch Black by Janeen Brian

Warp World by Heather Hammonds

The Soccer Expo by Sue Cason

Zit Face by Chris Bell

Goose Head by Wendy Graham

Big Day Out by Trish Lawrence

Getting Down and Dirty by Trish Lawrence

Real Guts by Jenny Pausacker

The Chilling Voice by Michael Dugan

Tank by Jenny Pausacker

Crash Landing by Dianne Bates